Humpback Whale Migration

by Grace Hansen

Abdo
ANIMAL MIGRATION
Kids

abdopublishing.com

Published by Abdo Kids, a division of ABDO, P.O. Box 398166, Minneapolis, Minnesota 55439.

Copyright © 2018 by Abdo Consulting Group, Inc. International copyrights reserved in all countries.
No part of this book may be reproduced in any form without written permission from the publisher.

Printed in the United States of America, North Mankato, Minnesota.

052017

092017

 THIS BOOK CONTAINS
RECYCLED MATERIALS

Photo Credits: iStock, Shutterstock

Production Contributors: Teddy Borth, Jennie Forsberg, Grace Hansen

Design Contributors: Dorothy Toth, Laura Mitchell

Publisher's Cataloging in Publication Data

Names: Hansen, Grace, author.

Title: Humpback whale migration / by Grace Hansen.

Description: Minneapolis, Minnesota : Abdo Kids, 2018 | Series: Animal migration
     | Includes bibliographical references and index.

Identifiers: LCCN 2016962362 | ISBN 9781532100284 (lib. bdg.) |
     ISBN 9781532100970 (ebook) | ISBN 9781532101526 (Read-to-me ebook)

Subjects: LCSH: Humpback whale--Juvenile literature. | Humpback whale
     migration--Juvenile literature.

Classification: DDC 599.5--dc23

LC record available at http://lccn.loc.gov/2016962362

Table of Contents

Humpback Whales

Humpback whales can be found in oceans around the world. A large group of humpbacks live in the North Pacific Ocean. These whales swim in the cold waters near Alaska.

Humpbacks feed during the summer months. The water surrounding Alaska is very **nutrient** rich. Massive humpbacks have plenty to eat.

Warmer Waters

Humpbacks travel to warmer waters each fall. Some North Pacific humpback whales swim to the Hawaiian Islands.

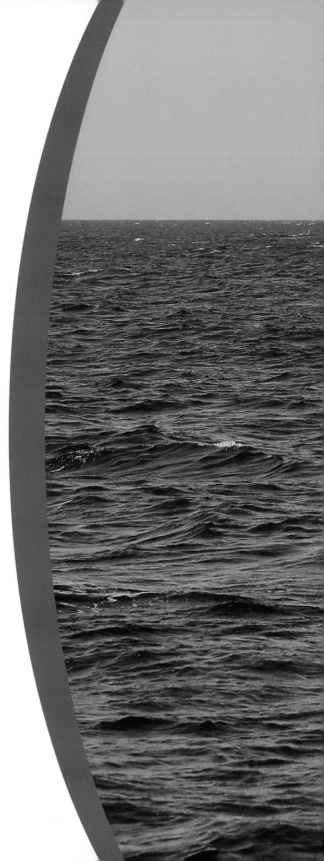

Alaska

Hawaiian Islands

This group of whales swims nearly 3,000 miles (4,828 km). Their long journey lasts 6 to 8 weeks.

Mothers and their **calves** are the first to arrive. Males and other females follow.

The last to arrive are pregnant females. They had to stay to eat a lot before swimming south. They need more fat on their bodies to fuel the long journey.

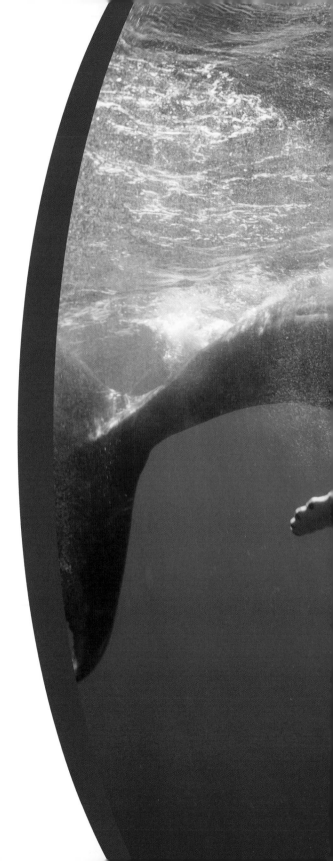

Humpbacks migrate for two main reasons. Whales **mate** in the winter months. Females also give birth in the winter. **Calves** have a better chance of surviving in warm, calm waters.

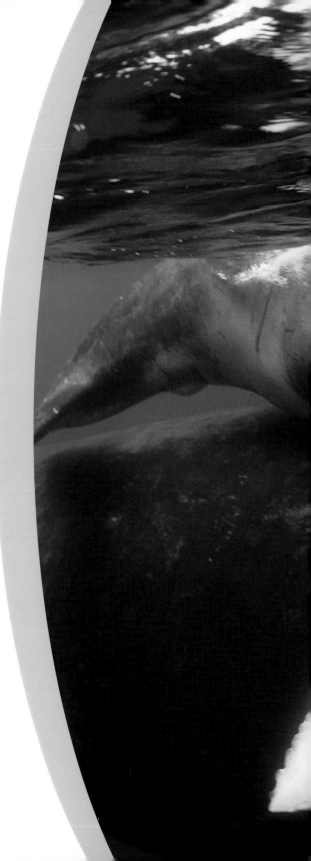

Humpbacks rarely eat in their winter homes. Their favorite foods are not found in **tropical** waters. During winter, they lose about 1/3 of their weight.

Back Home

It is time to swim back to
Alaska when spring arrives.
Humpbacks must go home
to feed for the summer. They
are ready for a big meal!

Humpback Whale Migration Routes

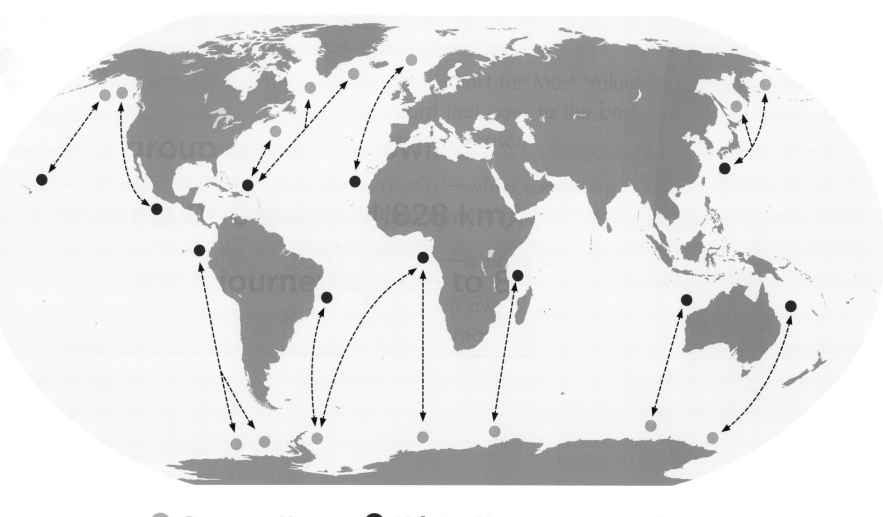

🔵 Summer Home ⚫ Winter Home ◀-----▶ Route

Glossary

calf – a baby whale.

mate – come together for breeding.

nutrient – a substance that is essential for growth and maintaining life.

tropical – a characteristic of a place near the equator with temperatures high enough to support plant growth year-round.

Index

abdokids.com

Use this code to log on to abdokids.com and access crafts, games, videos and more!

Abdo Kids Code:
AHK0284